Piano · Vocal · Guitar

IRISH FAVORITES

ISBN 978-0-7935-2176-0

HAL·LEONARD® CORPORATION
7777 W. BLUEMOUND RD. P.O. BOX 13819 MILWAUKEE, WI 53213

Piano·Vocal·Guitar

IRISH FAVORITES

CONTENTS

BELIEVE ME IF ALL THOSE
ENDEARING YOUNG CHARMS

Words by
THOMAS MOORE

DANNY BOY
(LONDONDERRY AIR)

Words by
FREDERICK EDWARD WEATHERLY

THE GALWAY PIPER

9

GARRYOWEN

1. Let__ Bac - chus' sons__ be not ____ dis - mayed, but__
2.-5. *See additional lyrics*

join__ with me__ each jo - vi - al blade come__ booze__ and sing__ and

lend__ your aid, to help__ me with__ the cho - rus. In-

Chorus:

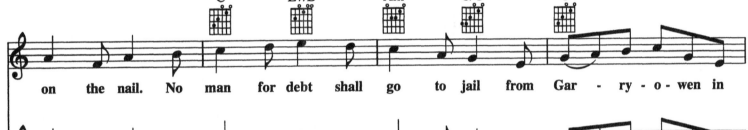

Additional Lyrics

2. We are the boys that take delight in
Smashing the Limerick lights when lighting.
Through all the streets like sporters fighting,
And tearing all before us.
To Chorus:

3. We'll break the windows, we'll break the doors,
The watch knock down by threes and fours;
Then let the doctors work their cures,
And tinker up our bruises.
To Chorus:

4. We'll beat the bailiffs out of fun,
We'll make the mayors and sheriffs run;
We are the boys no man dares dun,
If he regards a whole skin.
To Chorus:

5. Our hearts so stout have got us fame,
For soon 'tis known from whence we came;
Where'er we go they dread the name
Of Garryowen in glory.
To Chorus:

THE GIRL I LEFT BEHIND ME

I'm __ lone - some since I cross'd the hill, and
ne'er shall I for - get the night and the

o'er the moor __ and __ val - ley. Such __
stars were bright __ a - bove me, Such and __

heav - y thoughts my heart do fill since part - ing with my __
gen - tly lent their sil - v'ry light when first she vow'd she __

THE HARP THAT ONCE
THROUGH TARA'S HALLS

Words by
THOMAS MOORE

HARRIGAN

Words and Music by
GEORGE M. COHAN

HAS ANYBODY HERE SEEN KELLY?

Words and Music by C.W. MURPHY, WILL LETTERS,
JOHN CHARLES MOORE and WILLIAM J. McKENNA

Mich - ael Kel - ly with his sweet-heart
Ov - er on Fifth Av - en - ue, a

came from Coun - ty Cork and bent up - on a hol - i - day, they land - ed in New
band be - gan to play. Ten thou-sand men were march-ing for it was Saint Pat-rick's

York. They strolled a-round to see the sights a - las, it's sad to say, poor
day. The "Wear-ing of the Green" rang out up - on the morn-ing air. 'Twas

IF I KNOCK THE "L" OUT OF KELLY
(IT WOULD STILL BE KELLY TO ME)

Words by SAM M. LEWIS and JOE YOUNG
Music by BERY GRANT

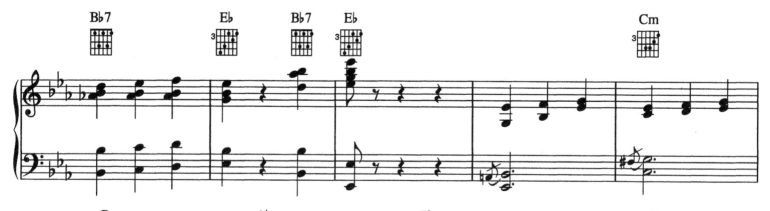

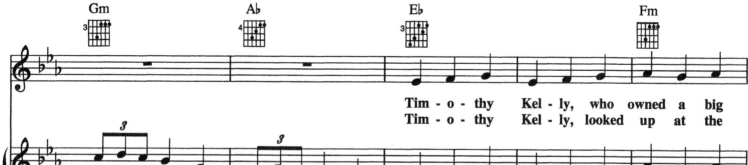

Tim - o - thy   Kel - ly, who owned a big
Tim - o - thy   Kel - ly, looked up at the

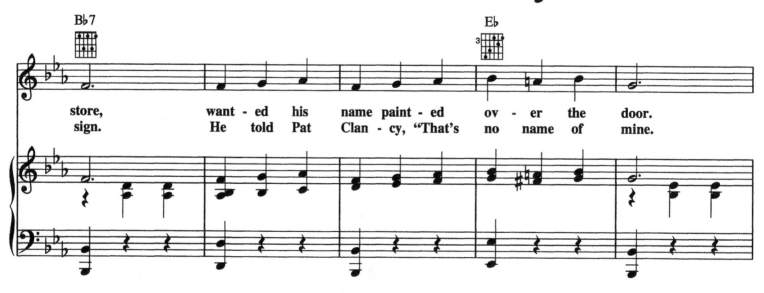

store,   want - ed his   name paint - ed   ov - er the   door.
sign.   He told Pat   Clan - cy, "That's   no   name of   mine.

THE IRISH WASHERWOMAN

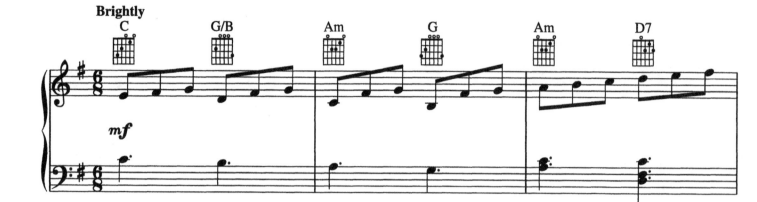

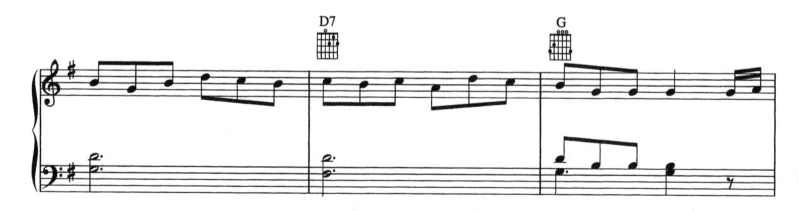

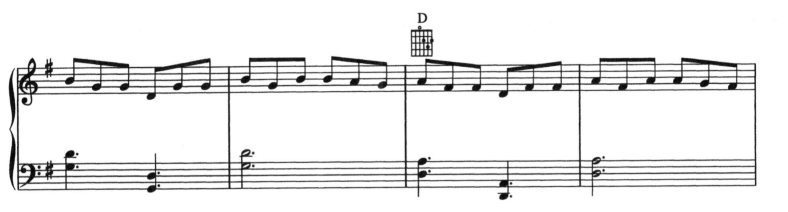

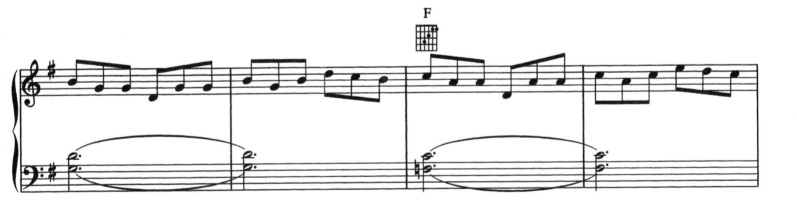

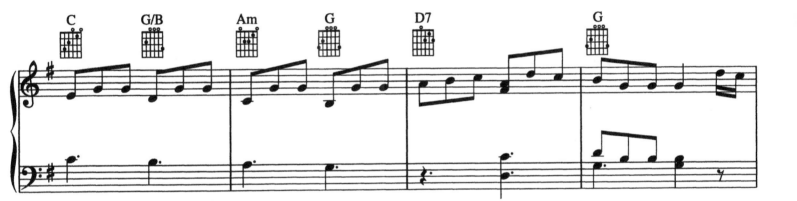

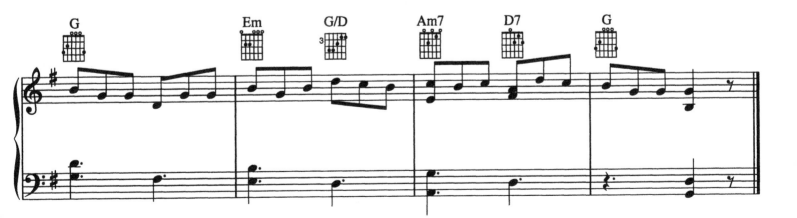

KATHLEEN MAVOURNEEN

Words by ANNIE BARRY CRAWFORD
Music by FREDERICK W. NICOLLIS CROUCH

30

THE KERRY DANCE

32

KILLARNEY

Words and Music by
M.W. BALFE

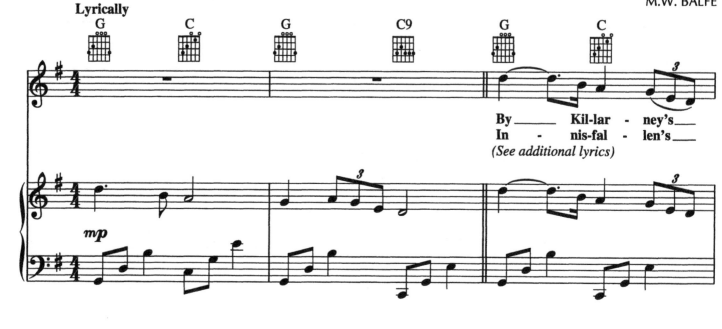

By ____ Kil-lar - ney's ____
In - nis-fal - len's ____
(See additional lyrics)

lakes and fells,   em - 'rald isles and ____ wind-ing bays,
ru - ined shrine   may ____ sug-gest a ____ pass-ing sigh,

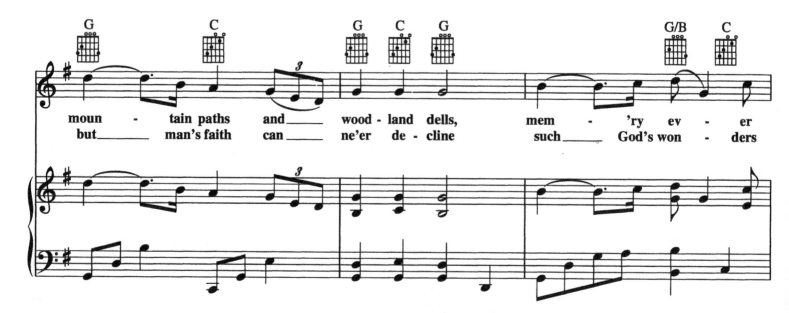

moun - tain paths and ____ wood - land dells,   mem - 'ry ev - er
but ____ man's faith can ____ ne'er de - cline   such ____ God's won - ders

Additional Lyrics

3. No place else can charm the eye with such bright and varied tints.
Ev'ry rock that you pass by, verdure 'broiders or besprints.
Virgin there the green grass grows. Ev'ry morn springs natal day.
Bright-hued berries daff the snows. Smiling winters frown away.
Angels, often pausing there, doubt if Eden were more fair.
Beauty's home, Killarney! Ever fair, Killarney!

4. Music there for echo dwells, makes each sound a harmony.
Many-voiced, the chorus swells 'til it faints in ecstasy.
With the charmful tints below, seems the Heav'n above to vie:
All rich colors that we know tinge the cloudwreaths in that sky.
Wings of angels so might shine, glancing back soft light divine.
Beauty's home, Killarney! Ever fair, Killarney!

KITTY OF COLERAINE

A LITTLE BIT OF HEAVEN
(SHURE THEY CALL IT IRELAND)

Lyric by J. KEIRN BRENNAN
Music by ERNEST R. BALL

42

MY WILD IRISH ROSE

Words and Music by
CHAUNCEY OLCOTT

McNAMARA'S BAND

Words by JOHN J. STAMFORD
Music by SHAMUS O'CONNOR

THE MINSTREL BOY

Words by THOMAS MOORE

MOLLY MALONE
(Cockles And Mussels)

MOTHER MACHREE

Words by RIDA JOHNSON YOUNG
Music by CHAUNCEY OLCOTT
and ERNEST R. BALL

RORY O'MOORE

56

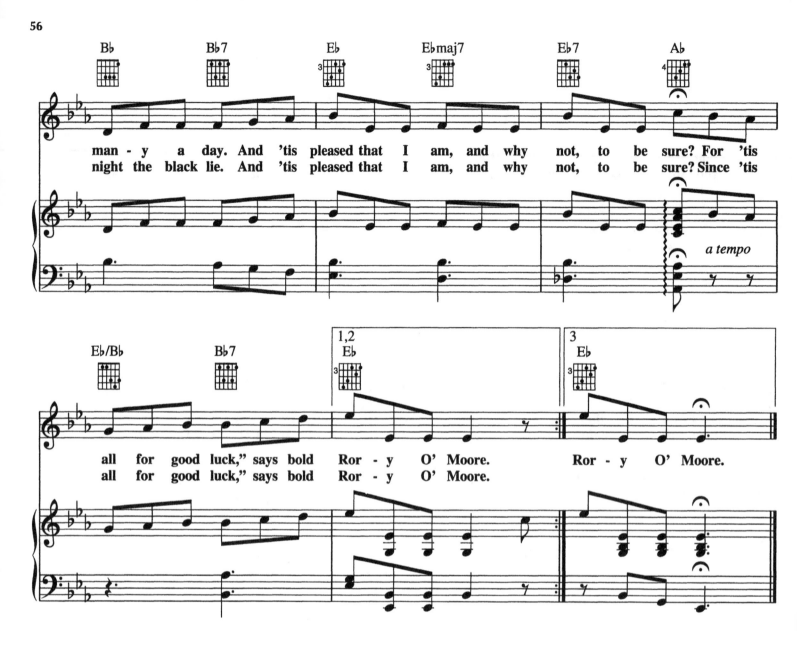

Additional Lyrics

Ah, Kathleen, my darling, you've teased me enough
and I've thrashed for your sake Dinny Grimes and Jim Duff.
And I've made myself drinking your health quite a beast
so I think after that I may talk to the priest.

Then Rory, the rogue, stole his arm 'round her neck,
so soft and so white, without freckle or speck.
And he looked in her eyes that were beaming with light
and he kissed her sweet lips. Don't you think he was right?

"Now Rory, leave off, sir! You'll hug me no more.
That's eight times today that you've kissed me before!"
"Then here goes another," says he, "to make sure."
"For there's luck in odd numbers!" says Rory O'Moore.

THE ROSE OF TRALEE

Words by C. MORDAUNT SPENCER
Music by CHARLES W. GLOVER

58

SWEET ROSIE O'GRADY

Words and Music by
MAUDE NUGENT

62

WHEN IRISH EYES ARE SMILING

Words by CHAUNCEY OLCOTT & GEORGE GRAFF, JR.
Music by ERNEST R. BALL

lilt of I - rish laugh - ter

You can hear the an - gels

sing._____ When I - rish

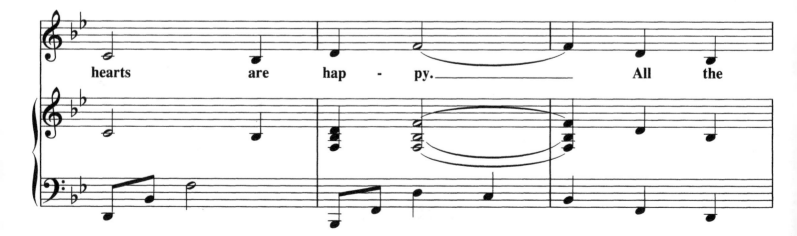

hearts are hap - py._____ All the

'TIS THE LAST ROSE OF SUMMER
(Air: The Groves Of Blarney)

Words by THOMAS MOORE

TOO-RA-LOO-RA-LOO-RAL
(That's An Irish Lullaby)

Words and Music by
J.R. SHANNON

TOURELAY

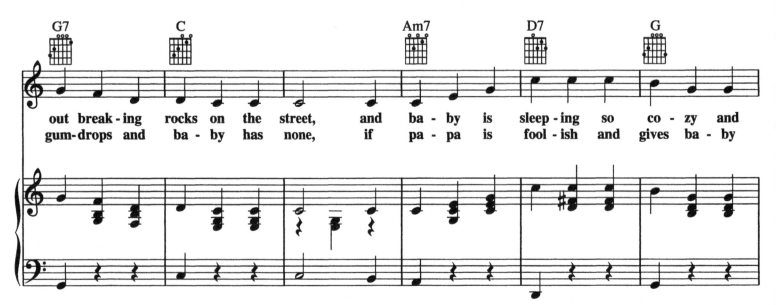

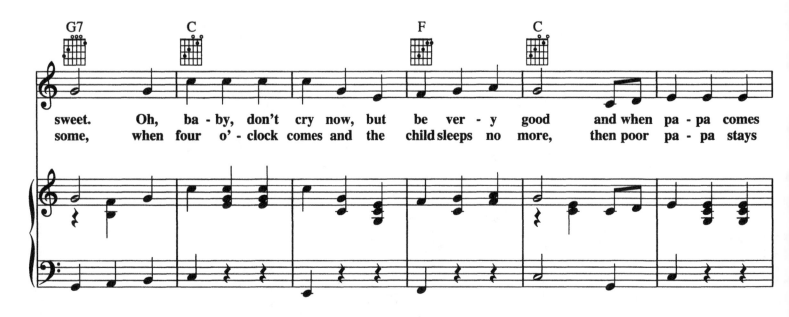

WEARING OF THE GREEN

Additional Lyrics

But, if at last our color should be torn from Ireland's heart,
Her sons, with shame and sorrow, from the dear old sail will part.
I've heard whisper of a country that lies far beyond the sea.
where rich and poor stand equal in the light of freedom's day.
Oh, Erin, must we leave you, driven by the tyrant's hand?
Must we ask a mother's welcome from a strange, but happier land?
Where the cruel cross of England's thraldom never shall be seen,
and where, thank god, we'll live and die still wearing of the green.

WHERE THE RIVER SHANNON FLOWS

Words and Music by
JAMES J. RUSSELL

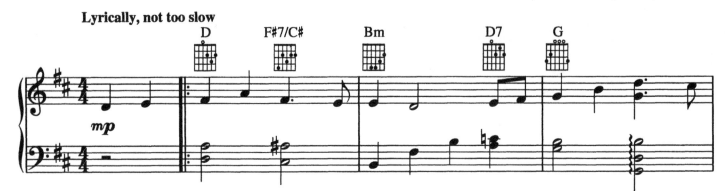

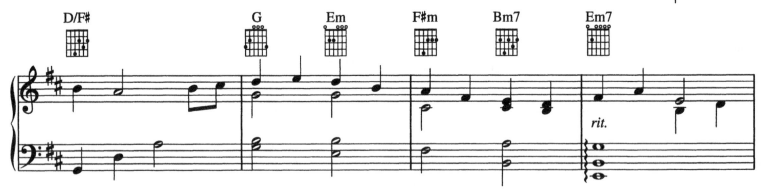

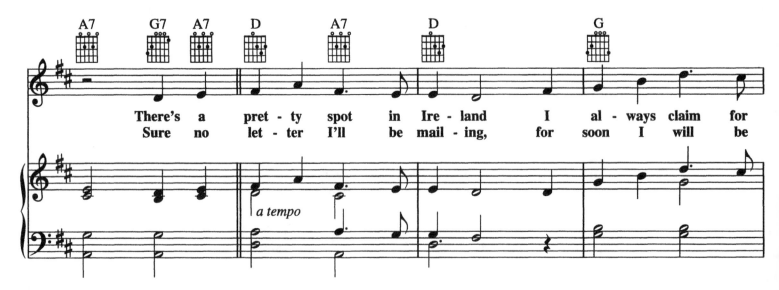

There's a pret-ty spot in Ire-land I al-ways claim for
Sure no let-ter I'll be mail-ing, for soon I will be

my land, where the fair-ies and the blar-ney will __ nev-er, nev-er
sail-ing. And I'll bless the ship that takes me to my dear old Er-in's

WHO THREW THE OVERALLS IN MISTRESS MURPHY'S CHOWDER

Words and Music by
GEORGE L. GIEFER

8va bassa

THE BEST EVER
COLLECTION
ARRANGED FOR PIANO, VOICE AND GUITAR

150 OF THE MOST BEAUTIFUL SONGS EVER
00360735 150 ballads..............................$32.99

BEST ACOUSTIC ROCK SONGS EVER
00310984 65 acouistic hits......................$22.99

MORE OF THE BEST ACOUSTIC ROCK SONGS EVER
00311738 69 songs..................................$19.95

BEST BIG BAND SONGS EVER
00286933 66 favorites $19.99

BEST BLUES SONGS EVER
00312874 73 blues tunes $19.99

BEST BROADWAY SONGS EVER - 6TH EDITION
00291992 85 songs..................................$24.99

MORE OF THE BEST BROADWAY SONGS EVER
00311501 82 songs..................................$22.95

BEST CHILDREN'S SONGS EVER
00159272 101 songs................................$19.99

BEST CHRISTMAS SONGS EVER
00359130 69 holiday favorites...............$27.50

BEST CLASSIC ROCK SONGS EVER
00289313 64 hits..$24.99

THE BEST COUNTRY ROCK SONGS EVER
00118881 52 hits $19.99

THE BEST CONTEMPORARY CHRISTIAN SONGS EVER – 2ND EDITION
00311985...$21.99

BEST COUNTRY SONGS EVER
00359135 76 classic country hits...........$22.99

BEST DISCO SONGS EVER
00312565 50 songs..................................$19.99

THE BEST DIXIELAND SONGS EVER
00312326...$19.99

BEST EARLY ROCK 'N' ROLL SONGS EVER
00310816 74 songs..................................$19.95

BEST EASY LISTENING SONGS EVER
00359193 75 mellow favorites...............$22.99

BEST FOLK/POP SONGS EVER
00138299 66 hits $19.99

BEST GOSPEL SONGS EVER
00310503 80 gospel songs......................$19.99

BEST HYMNS EVER
00310774 118 hymns $18.99

BEST JAZZ STANDARDS EVER
00311641 77 jazz hits.............................$22.99

BEST LATIN SONGS EVER
00310355 67 songs..................................$19.99

BEST LOVE SONGS EVER
00359198 62 favorite love songs...........$19.99

THE BEST MOVIE SONGS EVER SONGBOOK – 5TH EDITION
00291062 75 songs..................................$24.99

BEST MOVIE SOUNDTRACK SONGS EVER
00146161 70 songs..................................$19.99

BEST POP/ROCK SONGS EVER
00138279 50 classics $19.99

BEST PRAISE & WORSHIP SONGS EVER
00311057 80 all-time favorites...............$22.99

BEST R&B SONGS EVER
00310184 66 songs..................................$19.95

BEST ROCK SONGS EVER
00490424 63 songs..................................$18.95

BEST SONGS EVER
00265721 71 must-own classics $24.99

BEST SOUL SONGS EVER
00311427 70 hits $19.95

BEST STANDARDS EVER, VOL. 1 (A-L)
00359231 72 beautiful ballads...............$17.95

BEST STANDARDS EVER, VOL. 2 (M-Z)
00359232 73 songs..................................$17.95

MORE OF THE BEST STANDARDS EVER – VOL. 2 (M-Z) – 2ND EDITION
00310814...$17.95

BEST WEDDING SONGS EVER
00290985 70 songs..................................$24.99

HAL•LEONARD®
Visit us online
for complete songlists at
www.halleonard.com

Prices, contents and availability subject to change without notice. Not all products available outside the U.S.A.

0220
038